Heart's Symphony

Shikha Sharma Shah

BookLeaf Publishing

India | USA | UK

Presentation by *BookLeaf Publishing*

Web: www.bookleafpub.com

E-mail: info@bookleafpub.com

ISBN: 9789363311107

First edition 2024

DEDICATION

Dedicated to my amazing family ❤
And
To all the aspiring writers like me, you will make it big someday. Just believe in yourself!

ACKNOWLEDGEMENT

I would love to thank my close friend Barsha who brought my attention and interest in the subject of English when we were kids and also who shared with me her novels and wonderful vocabulary. Thanks for pushing me to speak my broken English then and for never laughing at it but rectifying me & for always encouraging me to get better at it. Super thanks to you for also helping me out with proof reading the poems in this book and helping me with the matters where required.

I would forever be grateful to my childhood friends who loved my writings then and encouraged me to continue writing more. Had you guys not praised me then, maybe I would have stopped writing at all. So today what I am is because of you all! Shruti, Vaibhav, Shally, Antika, Komal, Shayestah, Aranya and Mohana, I would love to thank each one of you. I would also like to thank my friends whom I met later in life, who gave me their true opinions about my work: Hardik, Bhavna, Nisha, Sandip, Jigar, Abhishek, Aditi, Dhwani, Kunal, Niyati. Thanks for being near or far, but always being there, my childhood buddies Aparna & Anjali.

I would love to thank my amazing English Teacher in college, Mrs. Sayantani Pal for raising my interest in writing proper poetries and for making me fall in love with the subject all over again! You have always been my inspiration. I would also love to thank my soft skill teachers Zubin Sir (who is also my current mentor), Jaideep Sir & Manish Sir for encouraging me to start writing my blog when you all saw my first piece of work which I understand must be quite amateur at the time, yet putting in that foundational belief in me. Thank you so much. Hope you all read this someday.

I would love to thank my dear husband Chidrup, my joy, my happiness, my partner-in-crime, my biggest support system, who has been my pillar throughout this journey and encouraged me to go ahead with this challenge. He has always had faith in me and my writings and always praised them with all his heart. Without his support, I might not have come this far. Thanks for giving me the wings to fly high and for respecting all my decisions. Also, thanks for always being the first one to read all my poems and share your viewpoints. Thanks for always trusting me even when I didn't trust myself. Thanks for everything and beyond Partner!

I would love to thank my dear friend and sister from another mother, Khush who despite having a super packed schedule took out time to proofread my poems and help me in this entire journey. She has been my push, always motivating me to be better, my light at the end of the tunnel, my cheerleader, my go-to person. She is the one who has stood by my side through all the thick & thin. Thanks Khush! I am forever grateful.

I would love to thank a very dear friend, Chetan, without whom this book coming to life wouldn't have taken place. Publishing a book was a faraway dream for me, the one that I hadn't even started dreaming about. Last year because of his push and persistence I could at least start thinking of the possibility of someday publishing a book. And here I am today, all because of him and his belief. Thanks for always pushing me hard to bring out the best in me.

Lastly, I would love to thank and shower my gratitude towards my parents for giving me this gift of life and for providing me with the best education that was possible for them, for always clapping hands and shedding that happy tear at the tiniest of my successes. You guys are my biggest cheerleader. Also I would love to thank my lovely In-Laws, Jayti di, Samir Bhai for always loving me and for giving me the freedom to be myself and soar high in the sky without obstruction. Without your love & support, nothing would have been possible. My super cool nephew Aadi, this one's for you!

Can't help but be super thankful to all the important people I mentioned above, you all make my life beautiful! Love you all loads.

Can't miss thanking all whose life has been the inspiration behind my poems. Thanks for giving me the subject to write upon.

Sorry if I missed anybody in the list above. Please know that I am thankful and indebted for having you in my life! :)

PREFACE

This book takes you through a journey on various subjects about life in general & about the emotional turmoil that one faces.

The book is divided into two parts, about nature & life, and about the emotional phases of relationship one goes through; pain, loss, being lost and at last rising from the ashes.

The poems are mostly raw as I write down my thoughts and feelings as they keep flowing, without much thought or interruption.

Being a sensitive person and a feeler, I strongly feel the emotions of others or my own self. And when the story of one becomes an inspiration or too much for my heart to hold on, then I write it down in the form of a poem.

Hope you relate to them & enjoy reading it!

-Shikha Sharma Shah

Moon

Beneath the clear black sky,
I see you, lovely and beautiful,
I see you right there shining bright,
Outstanding darkness around.

I hear various sounds nearby,
The chaos and the whispers,
The laughter and the chatters,
Yet nothing enters my mind.

I am so full of you,
That nothing around matters,
Nothing around makes sense,
Nothing around seems meaningful.

You always have a companion along,
Yet always distant too far,
Just silently admiring one another,
Making silent promises each night.

Just one look at you is enough,
For all the negatives to go away,
Your influence is so calm,
So mild, so peaceful.

I see the ocean across,
I see the lights around,
I see the beauty of the place,
Though nothing compares to you.

My view to you gets obstructed,
Time and again,
Yet I manage to steal one more glance,
Getting happiness unspoken.

Let's stay like the sea and the sky,
Never meeting yet always together,
Guiding through the way,
When the path seems too dark.

Fireflies & Moonlight

Sun scorching on my back,
Heat running through my veins,
Made me imagine something,
A world, one in my dreams.

As the eyes dropped close,
There it was right before me,
My world of imagination,
One where I want you and me to be.

I can see the violet skies,
I can hear the sound of the ocean,
I can see the snow on the mountain,
I can hear the winds blow across.

I can feel the serenity in the air,
I can feel the peacefulness in the space,
I can feel the purity of the white,
There was only calmness in sight.

There is tranquility all around,
People smiling & laughing,
A world with no tear or gain,
A world devoid of pain.

A world without greed for money,
One where all are equal & sunny,
A world where if one falls,
There are ten to raise.

A world that gets the best of nature,
The mountains, the ocean & the trees,
Where one can just sit & feel peace,
A place filled with cool breeze.

A world without judgements,
A world with brightness all around,
A world filled with happiness,
A world where freedom does the round.

A world where all coexist safely,
The animals, the birds, the humans,
A world where mermaids exist,
And so does the unicorn.

A world filled with love,
Where it is not questioned,
Instead looked upon,
With dignity & respect.

A place filled with waterfalls,
The coolness spreading everywhere,
Where there is no heat or cold,
Where it is pleasant all time round.
A world where there is equality,
Respect for the old, young & born,
A world believing in fairy tales,
A world trusting in serendipity & song.

A world which is not in a rat race,
A world where helping is the biggest trait,
Where empathy plays an important role,
Where every person is a winner of gold.

A world which is devoid of any war,
A world where countries bond,
A world where there is no ruler,
A world where all are free & bold.

A world where there are rains,
Of water & shooting stars,
Where every wish comes true,
Where no dream is far.

A world where there is no distinction,
Of caste, creed, colour or sect,
Where every living being is unique,
And has special power intact.

A world with daffodils, dahlia & lily,
With orchids, roses & sunflower,
Spread everywhere & beyond,
Spreading its fragrance in every corner.
A world which is painted in colours,
Blue, red, green & yellow,
And of all the bright colours,
Creating a painting on its own.

A world where death isn't painful,
Where every being is grateful,
A world devoid of diseases,
A world full of praises.

I want to live in this world,
Of imagination so bright,
Of love, happiness & laughter,
Of fireflies & moonlight.

Oh Himalayas!

I see you and get lost,
The most beautiful sight,
Filled with grace and might,
Absolutely perfectly imperfect.

Though invisible from far,
But once one gets closer,
There is no turning away,
There is no going back.

You lie within sheets of white,
Pure, Soulful and Serene,
Relaxing every single nerve,
All my senses feel at peace.

I get goosebumps seeing you,
How beautifully I feel,
Spirituality connected to you,
Joining holistic beads of life.

Being in your proximity alone,
Makes me feel closer to my soul,
It fills me with love and compassion,
With certainty of the uncertain.

You give me hope in the dark,
Despite the obstructions,
I can stand tall and high,
And face whatever comes.

You shine bright in the sun,
Making you look more majestic,
More charismatic, more appealing,
Attractive in the loveliest way.

Every time I want to run away,
All I feel like is coming to you,
You are my silence in chaos,
Oh Himalayas, the soul filler!

Canvas

Picture a beautiful canvas,
Right in front of you,
An image of the world around,
Sprayed in white and blue.

Thousands of emotions,
Just sprayed across,
Each denoting a meaning,
So pure, so true, so raw.

Beautiful bright colours,
Sprayed everywhere,
In different proportions,
In just the right amounts.

Sometimes more red,
Occasional popping up of green,
Moments of blue,
And lots of white.

Everyday brings about a new colour,
Sometimes a mixture of a few,
Sometimes nothing at all,
Sometimes all together.

It's how we deal with these colours,
How much importance we give,
To those positive shades,
How much we ignore the negatives.

Not that any colour is bad,
Or not required,
Since they teach us,
Necessary lessons of life.

To stay humble in the downfall,
To rise from the ashes,
To be happy no matter what,
To shine bright like a diamond.

To flow like water,
To burn like fire,
To stay grounded like Earth,
To mingle like air.

So just like nature,
Accept all the colours of life,
With arms wide open,
And paint a lovely canvas.

A canvas of you and me,
Of all the ones we love,
Of the ocean and the greens,
Of the mystic beings.
A canvas that speaks,
Colours that depict,
Emotions that flow,
To the eyes of the beholder.

Each day is a canvas,
Showing various pictures,
Of past, present and future,
All to be perceived in the best way.

We are the creators,
We are the doers,
We are the refiners,
Of this beautiful canvas called life.

Be the sunshine

The sun was shining bright in the sky,
Waves were crashing by the shore,
Trees were waving to the wind's lullaby,
Everything seemed perfect in sight.

There were faces around,
Nameless faces,
Speaking thousands of emotions,
Emotions not so bright.

She was sitting quietly,
With arms crossed,
Blank face staring at the horizon,
Thousands of thoughts in mind.

Her heart ached,
She smiled at the exterior,
And screamed loud inside,
Tears refusing to fall.

She wondered when shall it end,
When will she smile again,
Really smile from the heart,
Without having to fake around.

She wanted to feel happy,
The meaning of which was long gone,
She wondered if it was never ending,
The loop made her suffocate.

Worst of thoughts crossing by,
That foggy brain of hers,
Willing somebody to help,
Unwire all the mingling within.

There he was sitting shyly,
Conscious about the people around,
Angry that his parents planned this,
Coming here was not what he desired.

He wanted to go into the sea,
Splash the water,
Have fun like other kids,
Savour every moment of it.

The voice in his mind is loud,
It laughs at him,
Mocks him,
For the way he is.

He looks at himself,
At the extra pounds on his skin,
The one for which he is bullied,
Made feel terrible.
Nobody but he knew,
Of the condition he goes through,
Of the battles he fights each day,
Of the unsaid screams in his head.

She looked different,
Eyes distant yet close,
Speaking millions of words,
Unable to slip off the lips.

She was born this way,
With lots of innocence,
With nothing but purity,
Full of simplicity.

With the mind of a kid,
Blessed was she to never race,
In this mad world around,
Face the wickedness of it all.

Her parents worried,
Other kids made fun,
She was even mistreated,
Mistreated by her own.

Yes she was different,
With superpowers none had,
To feel others feelings,
To understand words unspoken.
Thousands such faces,
With stories of their own,
Silently fighting strongly,
Battles of their own.

If only the world was not cruel,
Wish it was filled with more empathy,
Filled with more love to give,
Filled with nothing but the good.

What if everybody's glasses was full,
So they didn't have to drink from others,
Making their glass vacant,
Leaving them thirsty and dry.

Love can heal the deepest of scars,
Smile can give courage infinite,
Genuine care can work wonders,
It can make a dying flower rise.

All are fighting within,
Some unsaid battle deep,
If only we uplift one another,
The world will be a beautiful place.

The scars on the outside are visible,
And has been getting treated for years,
Do not look at the scars of the mind as filth,
Treat it similarly as the physical.
Embrace everybody with affection,
Empathise with their situation,
Make them feel heard,
Make them feel seen.

And once we all join hands,
Healing shall begin,
There shall be lesser sad faces,
Lesser loss of lives.

Spread love,
Spread happiness,
Spread serenity,
Spread calmness.

It is contagious,
One help can lead to another,
One goodness can lead to another,
One ray of hope can lead to another.

So let's be that sunshine,
For people unknown and known,
Be their light in the darkness,
Be the change the world needs.

Runway

What is life but a series of take-offs and
landings,
Passing through the ebbs and flows,
Remaining static for the major part,
And then coming to a stop.

Teaching us major lessons in the meantime,
Giving us memories of a lifetime,
Sorrow and happiness going side by side,
Like waves of the ocean thrashing by.

Nothing is constant in life,
People come people go,
But the ones who remain,
Are forever and so.

People hurt unintentionally,
Forgiveness will set you free,
Letting go will be rough,
But that's what will make you tough.

Best friends swear togetherness for life,
And then they leave you in disguise,
Count your true friends on your fingertips,
Stick to them like glue too thick.
Love shall make you cry and moan,
They shall hold a special place till last dawn,
But scars too deep hurting like thorn,
Shall be a reminder of the pain you bore.

True love shall give you peace,
Thy shall be your relief,
Thy shall be your lost friend,
Thy shall be all you need.

Work with dedication,
Love with liberty,
Smile like a free bird,
Flying high with glee.

Family always sticks by your side,
No matter how hard you are on them,
Keep them close and never let them go,
They are your treasure, they are for life.

Detachments shall help you heal,
Keeping your heart sealed,
Acting like a parachute from falling,
Make sure you open it at the right toll.

In this world so huge and wide,
Stand up and protect yourself just fine,
Trust on none to do that at any pinnacle,
Be your own miracle.
Nothing is worth spending time on but yourself,
Try to find who you are, introspect your inner
self,
Life is too short to waste on negativities,
Be your own sunshine and moonlight.

Meaning of Life

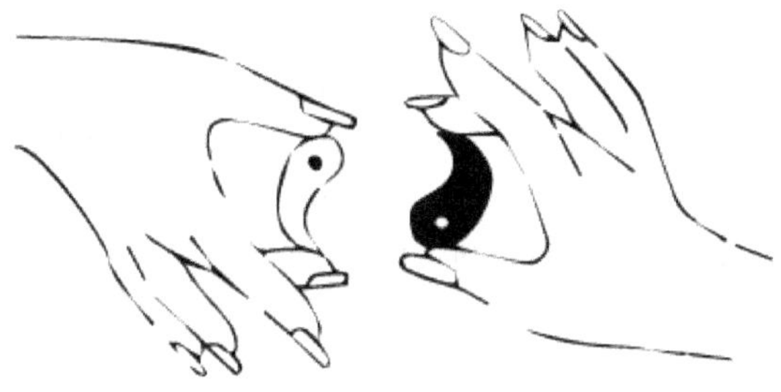

The crimson colour of the sky,
Seemed to quickly fade by,
Birds returned to their shelter,
Marking the end of another venture.
I sat there seeing the waves of the river,
Which seemed to revert in a quiver,
Thinking about the meaning of life,
Which now seemed like a game of dice.
Philosophies deep rising in my mind,
Leading to a lot of turbulence in disguise,
Serenity is all that I searched for,
Meaning of which seemed to have gone far.

Life seemed like a running race,
Where it is important to keep up with the pace,
Having no time to stop by and think,
Of all that we have lost just in a blink.
Spirituality now takes over my mind,
Path to which I am yet to confide,
Memories of the past flashes by,
And that's the moment when I hold myself tight,
Knowing that life has taken me ahead of time,
All I can do is weep and cry,
And then again stand tall,
Like a phoenix arising from the pyre,
All I want is to ponder for a while,
And to seek the meaning of LIFE…

Festival of Lights

There were lights and lights all around,
Not a smileless person to be found,
Festivity all around in the air,
People cheering everywhere.

She was sitting in a corner,
Watching it all hover,
People with crackers,
New clothes dapper.

Her heart told her to smile along,
To be in the moment, tag and go,
To derive happiness from others,
To be happy, without any bother.

She kept looking and gazing at them,
A site in the mirror of herself,
Reality came crashing to her,
All that's dark and with fear.

She wanted to scream to the world,
Why is it she who has to suffer,
Brink is what it seemed forever,
Money is nothing but delusion & grave.

Desire for new clothes rose in her,
But no penny in her pocket made her shiver,
No crackers for her like others,
Not any smile in her favour.

Careless rogues make her fear,
For her house of thatch may tear,
Looking up in the sky,
With those tiny hands and dreamy eyes.

It should make their hearts sink,
It should make their minds freak,
But there they are carefree & happy,
Living their blissful moment of joy.

She is just like you and me,
Just a girl wanting to change her destiny,
Let's together make her smile,
Let us all join hands & try!

'Happy'ness

Millions of faces in the world,
All running in the race of life,
In the process forgetting,
The true meaning of 'Happy'ness.

It is in the little things,
The little gestures,
The little fortunes,
The little cuddles.

It is in the blooming of a flower,
In the first ray of the sun,
In the waves at the sea shores,
In the snow on the mountains.

It is in the smile of our parents,
In the hug of our close friends,
In the cry of a newborn,
In the laughter of the elders.

It is in the kindness bestowed,
In the loyalty shown,
In the humble showers,
Of love and pleasure.

It is that calmness,
That serenity,
That excitement,
One feels on a new adventure.

It is in the awakening of the soul,
Listening to the preachings,
That brings us one step closer,
To our own self.

It is in watching,
The sunrise,
The sunsets,
And the moonlight.

It is lying in the grass,
And watching the stars,
Telling us several tales,
Of life and beyond.

It is in the stories,
Those little artifacts,
Of the old town,
Tell and expose.

It is in that music,
That we listen on loop,
That connects best,
To the deepest of ourselves.
It is in that painting,
That despite no words,
Telling us things unsaid,
Feelings unexplored.

It is in that dance,
That we flow with,
That helps us calm,
And enhance our senses.

It is on helping somebody,
Who has been struggling,
Without a hand to hold,
Being their strong support.

It is in seeing that lovely smile,
On the face of close ones,
On just looking at us,
After a long day.

It is stepping back on your bed,
Sleeping on your pillow,
After a long trip away,
Feeling the bliss of it.

It is in having the food,
Made by our mother,
With so much love,
So much affection.
It is in that tight hug,
By the father,
Whose everything lies,
In that one smile of the kid.

It is getting that warm hug,
By the long distant friend,
Having happy tears in the eyes,
Having lots to say and reminisce.

It is in seeing the newborn,
Smiling for the first time,
Holding our fingers,
Opening eyes with wonder.

It is not in materialism,
That all keep running for,
It is in these little moments,
Forming layers of 'Happy'ness.

P.S.: Here, according to the poet, Happyness refers to being in the most blissful and truly happy state from the deepest corner of the heart.

Same Page

Sunshine falling on my face,
Shining bright & beautiful,
Made me sit there and dare,
To think about things unsaid.

The voices echoed in my ears,
'Be the change you want to see',
Yet change needs to overcome fear,
To break the shackles and be clear.

Thousands of thoughts crossing by,
This inquisitive little brain of mine,
Fighting between the do's and don'ts,
Juggling between the right and the wrong.

Both were born quite the same,
Freedom screaming through their vein,
Then why their stories weren't the same,
Fate was playing a different game.

He certainly had extra privileges,
That she never felt she had,
He was devoid of the responsibility,
That strangely her shoulders tagged.

Why, why, oh why she cried,
To the universe above,
Why was she shackled down,
When he got to fly.

Why was she expected to behave,
In certain ways and boundaries,
Whereas he was allowed to reach,
For the sky and climb the trees.

Shouting and awakening the world,
To open their eyes wide,
To untangle the years-old beliefs,
To connect logic in their minds.

Both share the same sky,
Drink the same sea,
Tend to the same trees,

Live the same breeze.

Both are strong and capable,
Both are educated and smart,
Both have infinite power,
To wear every scar.

Then why oh why the distinction?
Why the levy of extra duties?
Why the incorrect expectation?
Why the implied responsibility?
Shouldn't there be equality?
A place where it can be either you or me?
Or a world where nothing is tagged,
Where one doesn't need to be sad.

Shouldn't both be taught empathy?
Shouldn't both be treated with dignity?
Shouldn't both bear the burdens?
Should one need to change all of a sudden?

The world is evolving and has changed,
Can't all try and put effort for the same?
Can we look forward, sit & gauge,
A day where both fall on the same page?

Lone Child

Sitting on the familiar bed,
She couldn't help but recall,
All the memories that drained,
From the broken sill of the window.

The rotten iron bars knew a story,
The river that flew below knew a few,
The trees below knew a zillion more,
Of everything she thought and far beyond.

She would sit there still for hours,
Wondering, thinking and interpreting,
Millions of thoughts crossing by,
That small incredible brain of hers.

She would talk to nature,
About things infinite,
About the mornings that turned into night,
About the distant lullabies & faraway cries.

Sometimes she didn't know,
How to deal with the world out wide,
She would escape the crowd,
To be there right by her own side.

She lived in a cocoon,
Unaware of the evil in the world,
But once she stepped out,
She knew there was no going back.

She struggled to face everything,
The emotional turmoil,
The vigilant faces, the tough words,
The mighty glares.

No matter how safe the cocoon felt,
The caterpillar had turned into a butterfly,
And it was time to face the world, unknown
A place where stagnant faces don't imply.

Time and again she would fly back,
To her safe place, to her cocoon,
Nobody taught her that it was time,
To bid her bye to the safe loom.

She struggled and fell,
Time and again,
Missing the river and the air,
Her window and the bed.

All she sometimes wanted was,
For someone to hold her hand,
To show her the way,
To sit there and just listen.
She wanted to set her mind free,
For that someone to have her back,
To entertain her wilderness,
And quest her inquisitive mind.

She wanted to learn things infinite,
To manage her turmoiled emotions,
To tell her what is wrong and right,
To be there for her with all might.

She tried to hold a few hands,
But they slipped away with time,
And there she was again,
Alone, for the downward climb.

Flying by that river she saw something,
A lovely reflection in the water,
And that's when she realized,
She was but filled with beautiful colours.

She didn't even know what hid within,
The beauty, the power, the strength,
The enormous generosity,
The magnificent heart of golden fate.

And in that moment she knew,
She was powerful enough,
She was brave to fight the worst,
She was strong to break her thirst.
She kept tumbling & falling,
Yet finding her way back,
Learning little by little,
About the mysteries of life!

Death

Serenity all around,
In the sheet of snow,
In the autumn leaves,
In the dry roses.

Peace like the Buddha,
Spread all across,
Magic as it felt,
Whiteness spread along.

There was calm,
There was peace,
There was tranquility,
All that I ever needed.

A bright light I remember,
Magnificent and tender,
Pulling me towards it,
For infinity and beyond.

Never felt that quietness,
Everything so cold,
Negativity was miles away,
'Happiness' as one told.

Nothing to worry about,
No sadness or fear,
No anxiety to cater to,
No suffocation or tears.

A herd of people,
Chattering along,
Having discussions,
Murmuring around.

So many minds,
Some brilliant thoughts,
Some fondly reciting,
Memories that last.

Faces many familiar,
Surrounded with love,
Minds clearly readable,
Eyes so gullible.

Now they face the truth,
The utmost superior truth,
Of life & beyond,
That remains constant all along.

Life is but a story,
Of a living body,
Filled with many chapters,
And ends at a point.
Chapters full of ups and downs,
Times of give ups & victories,
Filled with love & misery,
Full of agony & mystery.

Filled with pride & gain,
Sadness and pain,
Greed and ego stride,
Heart at constant fight.

Family against family,
Siblings against one another,
Moments of anguish & disruption,
Spread across like wildfire.

People seeking benefit out of the other,
Fighting for colourful pieces of paper,
They hold so close to their heart,
Someday which shall reach the Darth.

Not to forget the pleasant moments,
Ones filled with laughter adore,
Filled with smiles to treasure,
Happiness spreads across.

Yet now begins the spiritual journey,
To the absolute truth of all,
To find the reason for my being,
To free the soul from trolls.
There lies my body,
Quiet & sound,
Equal to nothing but the dirt,
From where it rose above.

Of to its onward journey,
Again with a baby born,
Filled with innocence,
And simplicity to adorn.

The soul found another cloth,
Of a different shape & form,
Hoping that this time it shall,
Find its true home.

My Sun & Moon

I look at you,
And find my entire universe there,
Right there in your arms,
Which holds me tight when I fall.

You have taught me to love,
To care,
To fight,
To dare.

You held my hands,
To show me the wrong & right,
You held me close,
When things went downright.

You fed me delicious food,
Compromising your own needs,
Never complaining about a thing,
Smilingly setting me free.

Sorry for all the time,
That I made you worry,
Not picking up the phone,
Or not listening to your screams.

You made me realise I had wings,
To soar high,
And touch the sky,
Bringing reality to my dreams.

You taught me to stand up for myself,
For nobody else would,
You taught me to survive,
In this bad world out there.

You made me laugh,
You made me cry,
You gave me lessons,
To last for life.

You sang me lullaby,
Holding me close,
You never let me cry,
Making way to all the smiles.

You made your entire world,
Around me,
Revolving time and again,
Coming back to me.

You came home all tired,
Absolutely out of energy,
Yet you would smile at me,
Making me laugh with glee.
You were my friend,
Turning all my discomfort around,
You taught me about the world,
Even when your own was upside down.

You were different from others,
You loved one and all,
Money never being a measure,
Of your wholesome simplicity & love.

You have the innocence of a child,
Ignorant of the workings of the world,
And that's what sets you apart,
From the horrors of the world.

You cried on my success,
You cried on my failure,
You cried at the moment,
My journey separated from yours.

Near or far,
Our hearts are entangled forever,
I am yours and you are mine,
Nobody in the world can change or lie.

I am born from your womb,
I have grown up in your arms,
You spent sleepless nights,
To keep me safe and secure.
Hope I can fulfill your dreams,
Making them all mine,
Hope I can give you the happiness,
That you both deserve.

Your lap feels like heaven,
Giving me all the peace of heart,
After I return home,
Fighting the battles of the world.

You raise me with so much care,
Differentiating right from the wrong,
Teaching me righteousness along,
Giving me lessons profound.

You love me with whole heart,
Treating me like your own,
Teaching me the value,
Of having you around.

You show me the path,
Like nobody else can,
Making me embrace spirituality,
In the purest form.

You teach me to be true,
Humble, simple & strong,
You are a living example,
God for us in human form.
Like the sun,
You brighten our life,
Like the moon,
You bring calmness and peace.

I feel immensely blessed,
To have such parents,
Grateful to the Universe,
For not just one but two.

May your smile never leave your lips,
May tears never reach your eyes,
I love you with all my heart,
My very own Sun & the Moon.

(Dedicated to both my parents and all the
fatherly and motherly figures in my life. Grateful
to have your blessings on us always.)

Home

Starring up in the void,
There are millions of stars,
And I could spot it there,
North Star, so close yet so far.

Like the moon is to the stars,
Like light is to the dark,
Like the key is to the lock,
Like a ship is to the dock.

Like waves are to the ocean,
Going its way away,
Yet coming back to it,
Finding its way back & stay.

What a warm hug feels,
After a long day ends,
What a forehead kiss feels,
Protective and with care.

What a gentle stroke feels,
With a head on their chest,
What holding the hand feels,
Filling the heart with sudden zest.

Looking at that face,
Brings relief and happiness,
Seeing that smile,
Brings peace unsaid.

What blanket is to the cold,
Utmost comfort is what you hold,
Saving from the windy day,
Saying words left untold.

How the sun feels in the winter,
Saving from the cold disaster,
How the soil smells,
After a shower of heavy rain.

There is a different strength,
Having you by the side,
A power untold,
To fight the worst of the sly.

What water is to a plant,
Without which survival gets hard,
What sea is to the sky,
Far yet always close by.

What a warm tea feels in the winter,
Giving comfort unspeakable & lither,
What a series of flowers feel,
Passing fragrance that lingers.
What that laughter means,
After a tough day of jitters,
When there is someone,
To wash away your tears.

What a soft song feels like,
All melodious and fine,
After a harsh morning,
Or a rough night.

How a match is to a box,
Discreet yet so strong,
Feeling safe there,
Capable of fire for long.

Always thought of four walls,
Being the place called home,
Made of bricks, cements,
Sand making it strong.

Yet now I know,
It is not anything material,
It is that special person,
The one I call my Home.

Friends

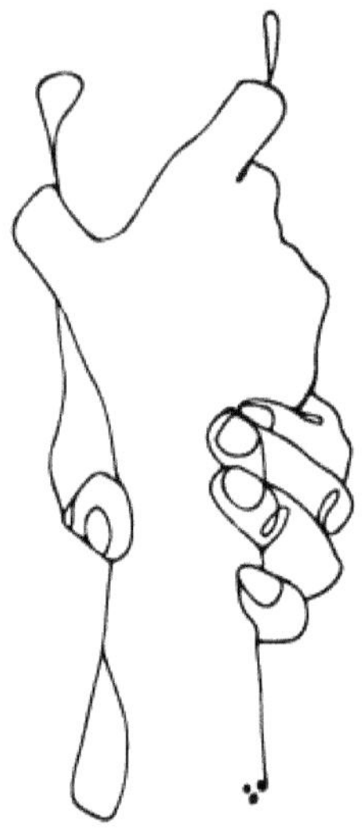

It could be seen from afar,
The carefree laughter,
The smiling faces,
Them holding hands.

Like two pods in a pea,
Like sand and the sea,
Like Cuckoo singing,
In a perfect symphony.

Silent supporters,
Ultimate protectors,
Secret warriors,
Biggest cheerleaders.

They never leave your hand,
Always having your back,
No matter how tough going gets,
They are right by your side.

Be it near or be it far,
No distance can separate them,
For no geography connects them,
But their soulful hearts.

They heal you from the pain,
Wishing nothing but your gain,
They help you fight each battle,
Less is what they do not let you settle.

Drawing various canvases together,
Painting it in colours bright,
Hand in hand they walk together,
For millions and millions of miles.

They protect you from yourself,
Bringing out the best in you,
They smile big in your success,
Happiness filling their heart.

They feel your pride,
Lower down your ego,
Keep you most connected,
Keep you more grounded.

They are your own,
The ones you never had,
You fight with them,
And love them harder.

You can talk to them,
Hours at stretch,
About lessons of life,
About stories unsaid.
They know your darkest secrets,
They know your deepest desire,
They push you one step more,
To fuel up that fire.

They know you inside out,
They know the depth of you,
They trust you hard,
Their faith stands apart.

They are your strength,
They are your weakness,
They are the pillars,
Of your multiple successes.

They save you from going astray,
They risk themselves for your gain,
They are the ones you fight for,
They are the ones in your very core.

Their hug is your biggest comfort,
Their shoulders being your support,
They are your best therapist,
Making you more optimist.

People call them friends,
I call them family,
For in every ups and downs,
We are in synchrony.
Blessed are those,
Who has true friends,
Keep them close,
For they are rare.

Love

Waves were crashing by the shore,
Taking routes unknown,
Breaking down the pebbles,
Looking up at the seagulls.

And my mind wavered to you,
I started imagining your face,
Imagine your hands holding mine,
Imagine my head on your shoulder.

An imagination that I had seen,
Not once or twice or thrice,
But many times,
In moments far away in time.

I could think of your eyes,
Silently looking at mine,
I could feel your heart,
Beating in the same rhythm as mine.

I could feel my heart flutter,
Words beginning to stutter,
I could feel the heat spread,
Across my cheeks so bright.

I could speak thousands of words,
Just through my eyes,
Knowing you will get them,
Without a hurdle crossing by.

I knew all your imperfections,
Embracing them quite fine,
I knew your limitations,
I knew your faraway cries.

And there it was so strong,
My urge to engulf it all,
To protect you from the harm,
You may get from any storm.

I imagine that knowing look,
In your bright wide eyes,
On listening to our song,
Or to the words known to you & I.

I can feel a sense of freedom,
Wings for me to fly,
To be nothing but myself,
Seeing me through your eyes.

With you by my side,
I know that I can,
Cross the oceans,
Touch the sky.
You push me to be better,
You push me to be strong,
You push me to be kind,
You push me to be a better me.

You tell me I have strength,
To reach the infinity and beyond,
To pass any hurdle or hustle,
To be forever limitless.

You are my friend,
You are my guide,
You are my favourite,
The one I want forever.

They ask what is love,
To me this is what it is,
To see togetherness with someone,
Forever in this life or another multiverse.

To just have them by the side,
In the moments of happiness,
Or in moments of despair,
To have them hold your hand.

Love is what sets you free,
What helps you grow,
What holds you tight,
Forever and beyond.
Love is worship,
It is a holy unison,
Of two hearts,
That beat as one.

It is a silent promise,
To be by each other's side,
To just be there always,
Till the sea meets the sky.

To hold hands and see,
Millions of twilights,
Gaze the stars at night,
See the sunrise.

To remove the line,
Between you and I,
Where we become reflections,
I become you and you become I.

They ask what is love,
A question so simple,
Yet with so many layers,
An absolutely intrinsic gem.

Faraway Cry

The path was lonely yet happy,
Living that way seemed not so crappy,
Two would make it merrier,
They said maybe even better.

Since long this quiet heart had seen a lot,
Seeking mercy from the lord,
Life couldn't be so unjust,
At a very young age, that child was lost.

Heart's palpitation was high,
Throat soaking up the cry,
Feeling the shattering of Dreams,
Giving out those silent screams.

A dream, yes a beautiful one,
Seen together was yet again broken,
Sight of a melodious change,
Was left unseen, unspoken.

A chance to pick up the broken pieces,
Was again snatched for prolong,
So many thoughts crossing my mind,
Seeking the answers to all the wrong.

Expectations of the laughter together,
All went in vain,
Leaving an aching heart,
Very hard and difficult to tame.

All the thoughts are jumbled up,
All the thoughts are drying,
Life is forcing me to break free of the fence,
Leave behind my trail of innocence.

Memories of the past flashing by,
Hurt panging again in my eyes,
Asking my own righteousness,
Asking if all I did was right.

A sound from faraway answered,
It has been exactly as it was written,
Need not shed a single tear,
For there is nobody to listen.

Become stronger than you were ever before,
Live the life that you deserve,
Maybe late, but not never,
For all the good things are always reserved.

Unforgotten

The light of the dusk,
Basking through the frame,
One of the best visions,
Turned out to be so painful.

The numbness ran over,
Every nerve of my body,
Pain seeping through the veins,
Tears hanging on the threshold.

The heart wants to be loved,
It wants to be seen,
It wants to be cared,
It wants to be felt.

Can one love someone so deep?
Can their touch be so important?
Can it be the reason for your survival?
Can it be the reason for your undoing?

The heart was tremendously aching,
Loving someone wasn't easy,
Yet breaking its high walls and borders,
Love found its way.

It felt unreal, surreal,
The happiness knew no bounds,
The lips couldn't stop smiling,
Mind couldn't stop thinking.

She knew it wasn't forever,
She knew it was one-sided,
She knew he would never feel it too,
Yet she chose to follow her heart.

And then the mirage broke,
She could see the land of illusion,
She could feel it so strong,
She broke, her heart broke.

There was no noise,
There was no sound,
Nothing but eerie silence,
And the broken heart.

More than her, her hope broke,
Hope that someday she will be loved,
The same way she loved him,
It faded away forever.

But the heart is so stupid,
It had engraved his name,
Right there at the center,
Forever and always.
How could that be removed,
How could that be undone,
He had become a part of her,
Unsaid, Unspoken, Unforgotten.

Broken

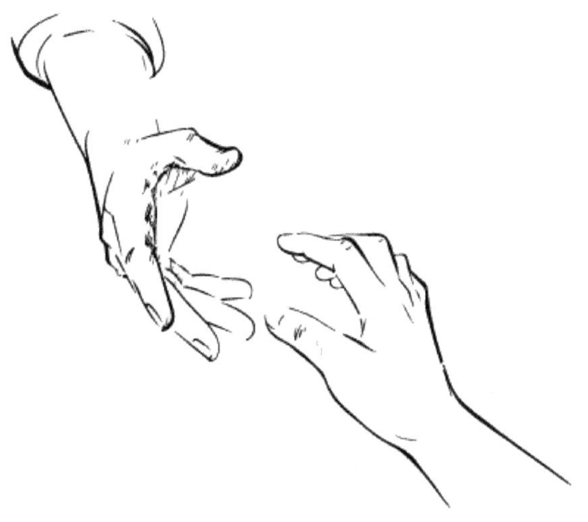

The broken glass and the empty vessel,
Spoke the stories of untold hassle,
Of Hearts broken and minds shattered,
Of feelings felt and so well altered.

The touch that felt like forever,
Disappeared without a waiver,
The smile that fluttered my heart,
Today didn't seem so right.

The feelings flowing through the eyes,
Was now gone and was sublime,
It all seemed so unreal,
It all seemed so surreal.

The dreams got broken into pieces,
The heart wasn't ready to get the thesis,
The laughter now seized to exist,
The tears now replaced and persist.

Making someone your world is easy,
But where to go when it gets breezy,
The urge to run away gets so addictive,
That everything else feels but vindictive.

The constant lump in the throat,
The constant fear of the unknown,
The constant feeling of missing,
The constant stab in the core.

The feeling of helplessness,
The feeling of being lost,
The feeling of suffocation,
Till when will it last?

Acceptance of the truth,
Seemed like a farfetched goal,
Gathering myself together,
Just trying to get on the roll.

Tug of War

Cold wind blows past my face,
Making me numb on its way,
Gathering every nerve together,
I hug myself tighter than ever.

Memories of the past keep flashing by,
Coming and going, shaking me within,
Not one soul to share it with,
In my very own prison of thoughts.

This love-hate relationship is tough,
The heart gets jumbled in every form,
In one moment you are the closest to me,
In the very next you are the farthest.

Sometimes I feel detached from you,
Sometimes so attached,
Sometimes I recall all our happy times,
Sometimes all I can think of are the bad.

You are the only one with whom,
I want to share every little thing,
You are the one at whom,
I want to scream at the top of my voice.

You are the one I want to,
Share words left unsaid,
My heart is scared,
For it may not stay safe there.

All I wanted was a best friend,
Love was never on the cards,
I am sorry that I fell for you,
Never knew it would tear us apart.

I miss that friend in you,
Who listened to my endless talks,
Who never judged me for who I am,
Who discreetly guided me the way.

I miss that friend in you,
Who made me laugh,
Who made me feel alive,
Who made me dance.

I want to run to you and talk,
So much about all that went wrong,
About all the knots between us,
To free them and bring us back.

Then there are moments when,
Love overpowers me,
And I take my steps back again,
To save myself from any pain.
Destiny is playing its roller coaster,
Emotions on the turmoil,
A constant tug of war at heart,
Juggling between peace and wry.

One moment I want to hug you tight,
Letting all the tears drain my eyes,
Other moment I want to push you away,
Saving us both from the hurt and pain.

There are times when I wonder,
Do you miss me at all?
Do you miss our laughter and talks?
Do you miss that friend you lost?

Then I bring myself back to life,
Trying to understand things infinite,
Considering you and your situation,
Distancing again to make things right.

I wish things were not complicated,
I wish we could freely remain us,
I wish things go back to normal,
I wish we get back to who we were.

Keeping every wish and hope alive,
All I want is for us to be happy and fine,
Maybe neither today nor tomorrow,
But someday, we walk again hand in hand.

Cage of my heart

I feel trapped,
Bonded up entirely,
By shackles unseen,
Shackles of emotions.

It's suffocating,
It's frustrating,
It's losing myself,
To an uncertain state.

My love for you,
Oh so overwhelming,
Your dislike for me,
So very shattering.

I am losing myself,
Slowly, steadily, gradually,
Towards an end,
That was pre-written.

In the process,
Rising and falling,
Learning and unlearning,
Lessons unsaid, lessons untold.

I can see your face,
Feel my love,
Know my limits,
And fake it up.

You are so important,
Yet so am I,
I need you,
But I need myself more.

Playing with the fire,
I have had my burns,
Yet every single time,
My heart still yearns.

Carrying these mixed emotions,
Has actually complicated,
The way things seemed,
The way things turn.

My heart is pure,
Filled with love and care,
Filled with innocence,
Not giving up till the end.

The journey is rocky,
The destination uncertain,
The path undiscovered,
The heart unattended.
Trying to break free,
My heart wants to beat,
Freely and happily,
Out of this prison.

Drowning

The depths of the water,
Was sucking me in,
Towards it with force,
That I had never felt before.

Breathing became difficult,
All I wanted was to give in,
I was tired of the strangle,
I was feeling in my chest.

I was tired of that shortage of breath,
I was tired of the suffocation,
I was tired of the constant pain,
I was tired of trying over & over again.

I wanted to let it go,
I tried too hard to float,
Gasping every breath possible,
Making every last effort.

Feeling of anxiety too strong,
Surrounding me with all black,
Fear of drowning on the rise,
Heartbeats craving a demise.

No sound in my conscience,
No reason to stay back,
No ray of hope alive,
No restrain from letting go.

So I succumbed to my pain,
Let go of the struggle within,
Released myself of everything,
Following the light beyond.

Phoenix

There is a haze of an image,
Image of you turning back,
Every minute detail of it,
Of that moment of the last bye.

That last moment of connection,
That last moment of laughter,
That last moment of smiles,
That last moment of us.

The sky seemed duller,
The winds felt colder,
The noises became louder,
The vision became blurred.

There was a moment of giving up,
Giving up everything good,
Giving up being happy,
Giving up feeling things at all.

But that was the moment,
When I became independent,
My happiness was no more tied,
Or bound to you and yours.

That last string had broken,
That last emotion was gone,
Yes there was a feeling of numbness,
But also filled with empowerment.

Gathering the strength to fight,
Fight my own helplessness,
Fight my own tears,
Fight my own emotions.

Suddenly there was a rush,
Rush of power,
Rush of self-reliance,
Rush of self-love.

Yes, memories kept rushing in,
Yes there were moments,
When I wanted to give in,
When the world ceased to exist.

But I had to rise above it all,
I had to face the world,
Eye to eye, shoulder to shoulder,
Making myself believe that I was enough.

Believe in nature and its timing,
To believe in fate,
To believe in the good in everything,
To believe it was all gonna be alright.
Maybe someday it will all make sense,
But for now, for today,
I am strong, capable and invincible,
Like a phoenix rising from the ashes.

My Shore

I was drowning in the ocean,
I swear I could feel it,
The suffocation in my breath,
The struggle in my beating heart.

I could feel my world crashing,
I could feel my lost willingness,
To hear one more word,
To feel one more feeling.

I had given up on myself,
And there you were,
Shining bright like the moon,
Spreading light in the darkness.

You gave me your hand in the ocean,
You pulled me out of the dark,
You gave me the courage,
To find the will, to give hope a start.

You showed me I too have wings,
To fly high in the sky,
To be my own master,
To be my own star.

You held my hand tight,
Through the tides low & high,
Bringing me to the shore,
Being there right by my side.

You told me it was alright,
To feel every emotion,
To stop shutting them down,
To listen to their tales & the unfelt cry.

To embrace myself completely,
With sides both black & white,
Realizing imperfection is beautiful,
Realizing it's after all mine.

You gave me the freedom,
To give words to my thoughts,
To connect back to my feelings,
Turning white into VIBGYOR.

You were there to ask how was I,
To sew up my feelings & agitation,
To listen to my endless talks,
To resolve my suffocation.

You told me it was okay,
To make mistakes & owe them up,
To not be hard on oneself,
To empathize with the flaws.
You taught me to stand tall,
For myself & for all the wrongs,
You made me face my traumas,
And how to hug them & let go.

You taught me to accept that sometimes,
It's okay not to be okay.
You taught resilience is power,
But not always.

You broke my societal norms,
That held me back tight,
You helped me to let go of,
All the guilt & pain I had tied.

You helped me push myself,
And outgrow to be who I am,
Taking life as it comes,
Welcome each day as a new one.

May you fly high & soar,
Climb the mountains, cross the shores,
Gain new experiences & grow,
Into a beautiful person whom I absolutely adore.

Love yourself

It was a perfect night,
A night full of stars,
Moon was shining bright,
Making it quite a sight.

Patches on the moon,
Visible on zoom,
Proudly showing its flaws,
Vision of imperfection it draws.

We are filled with burdens,
One of self-judgement,
Of wanting to be right,
To be the best in sight.

We empathise with others,
Removing their frights,
We pull them out from the wrong,
Turning them into a beautiful song.

An empty glass cannot pour water,
The glass needs to be full for the other,
Loving oneself should be a priority,
Before pouring it out in relatability.

Can we be kind to ourselves,
Like we are to others,
Can we not be hard on ourselves,
When things go wrong further.

Can we remind ourselves,
To build in self belief,
Devoid of false expectations,
Devoid of meaningless burdens.

Can we freely express emotions?
Can we allow ourselves to feel without notions?
Can we stop pleasing everybody?
Can we just be us without any worry?

You are beautiful,
You are complete,
You are extraordinary,
You are unique.

You deserve all the love,
All the care,
All the appreciation,
All the admiration.

Do not wait for anybody,
To shower you with love,
Fall in love with yourself,
Embracing you in all.
Fall in love with your limitations,
All of your mistakes,
All of your imperfections,
For they are after all yours.

You are human,
Born to make mistakes,
Learn from them,
And rise from the same.

It is okay,
Absolutely okay,
To feel any emotion,
To save your heart from extortion.

Prioritise yourself above all,
Be your warrior in every fall,
Hug yourself with love & care,
Falling in love all over again.

* 9 7 8 9 3 6 3 3 1 1 1 0 7 *